NEWFOUNDLAND SLANGUAGE

A FUN VISUAL GUIDE TO NEWFOUNDLAND TERMS AND PHRASES   BY MIKE ELLIS

GIBBS SMITH
TO ENRICH AND INSPIRE HUMANKIND

D1616147

DEDICATED TO SUZANNE, VIRGINIA, MIKEY, PHIDGETTE, DAISY, AND ROSEY

First Edition
23 22 21 20 19   5 4 3 2 1

Published by
Gibbs Smith
P.O. Box 667
Layton, Utah 84041

1.800.835.4993 orders
www.gibbs-smith.com

Designed by Michel Vrana
Printed and bound in Hong Kong

Gibbs Smith books are printed on paper produced
from sustainable PEFC-certified forest/controlled
wood source. Learn more at www.pefc.org.
Printed and bound in Hong Kong

Library of Congress Control Number:
2018963071
ISBN: 978-1-4236-5192-5

Special thanks to Katie Crane

Illustration Credits:
aarrows (gull, pp. 40, 87)
Aleks Melnik (nut, p. 8)
April Turner (gown, p. 34)
Arcady (balloon, p. 15)
Bakai (fin, p. 55)
bioraven (cap, p. 56)
Brian Goff (pie, p. 51)
Brovko Servhil (brick, p. 34)
Cattallina (duck, pp. 13, 77)
chotwit piyapramote (towel, pp. 15, 47)
D Line (screw, pp. 30, 93)
Ellika (apple, p. 46)
Gleb Guralnyk (bird, pp. 56, 96)
GoMixer (bridge, p. 93)
iconizer (cup, pp. 15, 45)
korsaralex (palm, p. 68)
locote (owl, p. 6)
lovedoves (yurt, pp. 9, 25)
musmellow (hook, pp. 21, 42)
NatBasilt (rat, p. 75)
natrot (ring, p. 77)
Rvector (broom, p. 84)
Sabelskaya (pig, pp. 66, 87, 95)
Sana7 (crown, p. 35)
tassel78 (pin, pp. 67, 83, 86)
Tribalium (write, p. 33)
Vector Tradition SM (saw, p. 86)
VectorShots (bat, p. 57)
Visual Generation (squid, p. 59)
VladisChern (spud, p. 27)
yyang (ape, p. 73)

CONTENTS

PREFACE

Many of the unique terms in this book are derived from the cod-fishing lifestyle of Canada's Atlantic seaboard that dominated the region for 500 years. It's been radically and forever altered since the late twentieth century because of overfishing.

In addition to providing a handy guide to pronouncing and understanding these Newfoundland terms, it's hoped that this book can serve in some small way to keep these words alive. They reflect a way of life that is fading away with each succeeding generation.

HOW TO USE THIS BOOK

If you're heading off on holiday to Canada's Atlantic seaboard with the notion that the natives speak the same English language that you do, this is the book for you! Just follow the directions below and soon you'll be able to say hundreds of words and phrases just like a native Newfoundlander.

• Follow the illustrated prompts and practice saying the phrase quickly and smoothly.

• Emphasize the words or syllables highlighted in red.

• A strikethrough means you don't pronounce that letter or letters.

• Learn to string together words or phrases to create many more phrases.

• Draw your own pictures to help with memorization and pronunciation.

Note: This book may produce an Americanized version of Newfoundland English.

For free sound bytes, visit slanguage.com.

How are you,
my friend?
*'Ow's she cuttin',
me cocky?*

Owl's She Cut'n Me

Cod Key?

How are you
getting on?
'Ow's she gettin' on?

Owl's She Get'n On?

Great!
Best kind, b'y!

Best Kind Buy!

Yes I am
'Deed I is

Deed Eye Is

What's up?
Whadda ya at?

Woody At?

What just happened?
*What's after
happening now?*

Watts After Hap

Nin Now?

Nothing much
Nuttin', b'y

Nut'n Buy

Where are you from?
Where you 'longs to?

Wear U Longs 2

Who are your parents?
Who knit ya?

Who Nit Cha?

I'll be right over
I'll be over now, d'once

All Bee Over Now

Duh Once

I'll put the kettle on
I'll put da ol' slut on

All Put Duh Old Slut On

You know it's true
You knows yourself

U Nose Yurt Self

Go on, really?
G'wan, b'y!

G'wan Buy!

Whatever
What odds

What Odds

Forget it
Shag it

Shag It

Don't do that
Don't be at it

D'Own Bee Add It

Get away
Get clear

Get Claire

Long may your
fortunes last
*Long may your
big jib draw*

Long Mayor Big Jib

Draw

FAMILY, FRIENDS, AND OTHER FOLK

Father
Fadder

Far Dirt

Mother
Mudder

Mud Dirt

Friend
B'y

Buy

Sweetie
Ducky

Duck Key

My old chum
Me ol' trout

Me Old Trout

My love
My treasure

My Treasure

Mischievous young boy
Laddio

Lad Eee Oh

Mischievous child
Nointer

Annoint Turn

Bully
Cockabaloo

Cock Cup Balloon

Jinx
Jinker

Jing Curb

From St. John's
Townie

Towel Knee

From anywhere in
Newfoundland other
than St. John's
Bayman

Bay Min

Not from
Newfoundland
Come from away

Come From Uh Weigh

Come from away
CFA (acronym)

See Eff Ace

Braggart
Maw-mouth

Mom Mouth

Hoodlum
Skeet

Ski't

Idler
Nunny-fudger

Nun Knee Fudger

Jerk
Scut

S'Cut

Loafer
Noody-nawdy

New Deed Naughty

Loudmouth
Bullamarue

Bull Uh Maroon

Mess
Streel

St'Reel

Scalawag
Tallywack

Tally Wack

Scoundrel
Sleeveen

Sleeve Een

Simpleton
Gommel

Gong Mull

Slob
Slawmeen

Slum Mean

Sluggard
Hangashore

Angus Shore

Wastrel
Futter

Fud Dirt

Whiner
Sook

S'Hook

Wimp
Nish

Nish

Abuse
Ballyrag

Bally Rag

Shoe'll

Back away
Shule

Break off
Snop

Snop

Claw
Scrawb

Sk'Rob

Clean thoroughly
Scurrifunge

Skirt Rough Grunge

Crouch down
Coopy down

Coop Pea Down

Dance
Wallop

Wall Up

Go somewhere
Muck off

Muck Off

Grasp the meaning
Twig

Twig

Guzzle
Guttle

Gudd'll

Honk (car horn)
Barmp

Burmp

Hurt
Smert

Sm'Yurt

Joke
Skit

Skit

Leave
Leff

Left

Lie down
Keel

Keel

Meander
Marl

M'Earl

Mess up
Caudle up

Cod'll Up

Mix
Mang

Mang

Muddle
Spuddle

Spud'll

Nip
Yop

Yop

Pack tightly
Chinch

Chinch

Play hooky
(from school)
Pip off

Pip Off

Rectify
Rightify

Right If Eye

Retort
Yap

Yap

Saunter
Sog along

Sog Uh Long

Scrimp
Naggle

Nag'll

Shiver
Bivver

Bivver

Snatch
Glom

Glom

Squash
Squat

Squat

Squat
Quat

K'Watt

Squeak
Scroop

Screw'p

Swallow
Glutch

Glutch

Thrash
Drash

D'Rash

Toss
Bazz

Bazz

Turn around
Sloo

Slew

Window shop
Twack

Twack

ADJECTIVES AND ADVERBS

Across from
Overright

Over Write

After
Apast

Up Past

Annoyed
Rotted

Rotted

Askew
Asquish

Us Squish

Awkward
Gowdy

Gown Dee

Be there right away
Be there da once

Bee There Duh Once

Behind
Aback

Up Back

Brittle
Brickly

Brick Lee

Cantankerous
Crousty

Crown Steed

Congested (nose)
Snowchy

Snout Cheese

Cranky
Crooked

Crooked

Crooked
Squish

Squish

Equitable
Jonnick

John Ick

Cow'd Out

Exhausted
Cowed out

Fidgety
Flicy

Fly See

Flabby
Squabby

Squaw Bee

Hapless *Lewerdly*	**Lou Word Leek**
Happy-go-lucky *Jack-easy*	**Jack Easy**
Hungry *Leery*	**Leery**
Ill-tempered *Biniky*	**Bin Icky**

Irked
Huffed

Huff'd

Later on
Bumbuy

Bum Buy

Lavish
Flahoolach

Flood Hoop Lick

Misty
Mauzy

Ma Zee

Musty
Fousty

Faust Tee

None
Nar

Gnarly

Plenty
Lashins

Lash Inns

Pretty close
Paddy keefe

Patty Key'f

Rowdy
Wrangle-gangle

Rang Gull Gang Gull

Satiated
Stogged

Stogg'd

Scrawny
Rawny

Raw Knee

Sickly
Dishy

Dish She

Slimy
Slubby

Slub Bee

Slovenly
Slommocky

Slum Icky

Soaking wet
Sached

Satchel

Stolen
Bucked

Buck'd

Thawed out
Slacked up

Slack'd Up

Wary
Yary

Yacht Reed

Whiny
Sooky

S'Hook Key

Do you want
something to eat?
*Do you want some
taken up?*

D'Ya Want Sum

Taken Up?

I'm starving
*I'm just 'bout
gut-foundered*

Eye'm Juss Bout Gut

Found Dirt

Make something to eat
Cook up a scoff

Cook Cup Us Scoff

Snack
Boil up

Boil Up

Coffee break
Mug up

Mug Up

Bar food
Grog bits

Grog Bits

Boiled cod and
hardtack
Fish 'n' brewis

Fishin' Bruise

Cloudberries
Bakeapples

Bake Apples

Crispy fried pork fat
Scrunchions

Scrunch Inns

Dumpling
Doughboy

Dough Boy

Fish stew with
potatoes and onions
Lobscouse

Lob Scows

Fried bologna
Newfie steak

New Fee Steak

Fried bread dough
Touton

Towel'tn

Grub
Prog

Prog

Hardtack
Sea biscuit

 See Biscuit

Jam sandwich cookie
Jam jams

Jam Jams

Leftovers
Couldn'ts

Couldn'ts

Lingonberry
Partridgeberry

Part Ridge Berry

Molasses
Lassy

Lass See

Molasses buns
Khaki dodgers

Cat Key Dodgers

Molasses pancake
Gandy

Gan Dee

Molasses-sweetened tea
Switchel

Switch'll

Pancake
Bangbelly

Bang Belly

Pea porridge
Pease pudding

Peas Puddin'

Pig's head terrine
Brawn

Brawn

Porridge
Mush

Mush

Seal flipper meat pie
Flipper pie

Flipper Pie

Spiced pudding
with raisins
Figgy duff

Fig Eee Duff

Spicy candied fruit
cookies
Lassy mogs

Lass See Mogs

Steamed pudding
Duff

Duff

Sunday dinner of
boiled beef and veggies
Jiggs dinner

Jigs Dinner

Unleavened biscuits
Flummies

Flum Ease

Away from your
current location
(in any direction)
Up the shore

⬆ **Up The Shore**

Down the shore

Down The Shore

Up along

⬆ **Up Along**

Further down the
coast
Down the arm

Down Thee Arm

Deep wooded valley
Drook

D'Rook

Narrow rocky lane
Drung

D'Rung

Newfoundland
Newfoundland

New Fin Land

Brigus
Brigus

Brig Us

Burgeo
Burgeo

Bird Geo

Cappahayden
Cappahayden

Cap Uh Hay Dun

Come by Chance
Come by Chance

Come Buy Chance

Cupids
Cupids

Cue Pids

Fogo Island
Fogo Island

Foe Go Eye Lund

Griquet
Griquet

Grip Kit

Gros Morne
Gros Morne

Gross Mourn

Joe Batt's Arm
Joe Batt's Arm

Joe Bats Arm

Kittiwake
Kittiwake

Kitty Wake

L'Anse aux Meadows
L'Anse aux Meadows

Lance Sum Med Doze

Quidi Vidi
Quidi Vidi

Kitty Video

Quirpon
Quirpon

Car Poon

St. John's
St. John's

Sin Johns

Skerwink Trail
Skerwink Trail

Scurry Wink Trail

Squid Tickle
Squid Tickle

Squid Tickle

Tilting
Tilting

Till Ting

Torngat Mountains
Torngat Mountains

Torn Gat Mountains

Twillingate
Twillingate

Twill Inn Gate

Wabana
Wabana

What Bond Uh

Witless Bay
Witless Bay

Wit Liss Bay

Accordion
Cardeen

Car Dean

Card game
120s

Uh Hun Dirt'n Twenties

Children's play house
Cubby house

Cub Bee House

Dinner and dancing
Scoff and a scuff

Scoff En Us Scuff

Game played with
sticks
Tiddly

Tid Lee

Good time at a party
Lawnya vawnya

Lawn Yum Von Yum

Marbles
Alleys

Al Ease

Ready or not, here
I come!
*Hoist your sails
and run!*

Heist Yer Sells En Run!

BIRDS, BUGS, AND OTHER BEASTIES

Ant
Emmet

Em Mitt

A kind of baitfish
Caplin

Cape Lynn

Butterfly
Pitchy-paw

Pit Cheap Paw

Small, yappy dog
Cracky

Crack Key

Flea
Lop

Lop

Puff Pig

Harbor porpoise
Puff-pig

Lass See Bug

Ladybug
Lassy bug

Nipper

Large mosquito
Nipper

Moth
Dows'y poll

Down Zee Paul

Murre (seabird)
Turr

Turn

Seal
Swile

S'While

Sow bug
Carpenter

Car Pin Turn

Wasp
Wop

Wop

Woolly bear caterpillar
Hairy palmer

Hairy Palm Her

A SAILOR'S LIFE FOR ME

Boatload of fish
Sagger

Sagger

Coastal lagoon
Barrisway

Embarass Sway

Covered space in
a boat's bow
Cuddy

Cuddy

Dangerous floating
ice chunk
Growler

Growler

Doldrums
Dilly-dalls

Dill Lee Dalls

Empty fish trap
Water haul

Water Hall

Fish slime
Slub

Slub

Frozen sea spray
Ballycater

Bally Kay Turn

Heavy seas
Roughery

Rough Furry

Large waves
Tumbly

Tum Bleed

Lighthouse
Lume

Loom

Mooring post
Grump

Grump

Mooring rope
Frape

Fr'Ape

Newly frozen ice
Slob

Slob

No fish
Nar fish

Gnarly Fish

Patch on a boat
Teeveen

Tee Veen

Small breaking waves
Lops

Lops

Small chunks of ice
Bergy bits

Burg Eee Bits

Small round-bottom
boat
Rodney

Rod Knee

Soft harbor ice
Lolly

Law Lee

Stone or wooden
anchor
Killick

Kill Lick

Thin, slushy ice
Sish

Sish

Three-handed punt
High rat

Hi Rat

WEATHERING THE STORM

Blustery
Faffering

Fat Fur Ring

Brief snow shower
Dwai

D'Why

Dusk
Duckish

Duck Fish

Exceptionally cold
Cold enough to clip ya

Cold Enough 2 Clip Yuh

Frozen
Frore

Fr'Oar

Ice formed from
freezing rain
Glitter

Glitter

Misty rain
Misk

Misk

Overcast and gloomy
Grum

Grum

Picture-perfect
weather
Pet day

Pet Day

Rain, drizzle, fog
RDF (acronym)

Arm Deed Eff

Sheltered from
the wind
In the lun

Inn The Lunch

Squall
Scad

Scad

Stormy
Knotty

Naughty

Thin ice
Nish ice

Nish Ice

Threatening weather
Weatherish

Weather Fish

Braids
Plats

Plats

☆

Buttocks
Starn

Star'n

Head
Nopper

Nopper

Knee
Knuck

Nuck

Mouth
Gob

Gob

Phlegm
Glander

Glander

Pregnant
*Something under
your pinny*

Sum Thin Under Yer

Pin Knee

Scratch (small wound)
Scrawb

Sk'Rob

Stomach
Puddock

Pud Ick

Unkempt hair
Birch broom in the fits

Birch Broom Inn the Fitz

Apron
Pinny

Pin Knee

Best Sunday shoes
God walkers

God Walkers

Big rubber boots cut
off at the ankle
Sawboos

Saw Boo's

Crotch of trousers
Ferks

Fur'ks

Extra-padded mitten
Thrum mitt

Thrum Mitt

Fingerless mitten
Cuff

Cuff

Gaiter
Hoggelly bog

Hog Gull Eee Bog

Heavy sheepskin
jacket
Lammy

Lamb Me

Leather bootlace
Fong

Fong

Oilskin fishing hat
Linkum

Link Um

Overcoat
Banger

Banger

Shawl
Spanker

Spanker

Shoe soles
Taps

Taps

Short, thick oversock
Vamp

Vamp

Soft untanned hide shoe
Pampooty

Pam Poo Tee

BITS AND BOBS

Bundle of firewood
Faddle

Fad'll

Ceremony for
honorary
Newfoundlanders
Screech-in

Screech Inn

Fence rails
Longers

Longers

Floor
Planken

Plank'n

Foolish saying
Quism

Kizz Um

Goofing off
Whizgigging

Whiz Gigging

Nightmare vision
Old hag

Old Hag

Nightmares
Diddies

Did Ease

Nonsense
Fiddle faddle

Fit'll Fad'll

Penny-pincher
Scroople

Screw Pull

Porch
Bridge

Bridge

Small tin cup
Bannikin

Ban Uh Kin

Sparks
Flankers

Flankers

Speck
Peck

Peck

Stain
Smidge

Smidge

State of confusion
Confloption

Cun Flop Shun

Stink
Hum

Hum

Superstition
Pishogue

Pish Hog

Tea kettle
Hurry-up

Hurry Up

Thingamajig
Chummy

Chum Me

Untidy mess
Clobber

Claw Bird

A whole bunch
(of something)
Yaffle

Yaff Full